Selected Poems

Also by David Wright

To the Gods the Shades:
Collected Poems

DAVID WRIGHT
SELECTED POEMS

CARCANET

First published in 1988 by
Carcanet Press Limited
208-212 Corn Exchange Buildings
Manchester M4 3BQ

Copyright © 1988 David Wright
All rights reserved

British Library Cataloguing in Publication Data

Wright, David, *1920-*
  Selected poems.
  I. Title
  821'.914

  ISBN 0-85635-753-7

The publisher acknowledges financial assistance
from the Arts Council of Great Britain

Typeset in 10pt Palatino by Bryan Williamson, Manchester
Printed in England by SRP Ltd, Exeter

Contents

Five South African Poems	7
On Himself	11
Canons Ashby	12
On the Death of an Emperor Penguin in Regent's Park	13
Moral Stories	14
A Funeral Oration	18
Monologue of a Deaf Man	19
An Invocation to the Goddess	21
Adam at Evening	22
Rhapsody of a Middle-aged Man	24
At a Café Table	26
A Visit to the Protestant Cemetery	28
By the Effigy of St Cecilia	29
Campo Santo	30
Kleomedes	32
Plettenberg's Bay	35
On the Margin	38
A Cemetery in Dumfriesshire	43
Chester Car Park	44
The Lakes	45
Grasmere Sonnets	46
The Deviser	48
Words	49
Swift	51
Rook	52
E.P. at Westminster	54
On a Friend Dying	55
A Peripatetic Letter to Isabella Fey	57
Bom Jesus	65
Encounter	67
Balloon	68
The Musician	69
Procession	70
Cockermouth	71

Five Songs	73
Notes on a Visit	77
Beeches	81
Images for a Painter	82
Prospects	85
An Elegy	94

Five South African Poems
for Arthur Oldham

I

Each time I return to Johannesburg it is summer,
And clouds hang with black the stage of the sky,
So I perceive the auditors prepared for tragedy,
Ready for lightning, where a harp of thunder

Leans towards Magaliesberg. Does my childhood
Lie before those mountains, where Pretoria
Veils her white façades with jacaranda
Below their shoulders? From Orange Grove

I'd look all the morning at the distance laid between,
The bare areas, undeveloped altitudes,
And plant their furlongs with imagined woods
To be grown in the fields between Magaliesberg and my home.

Over them stoop and bend the throats of summer
Each time I return to Johannesburg. Over them
I see and hear a portentous requiem
Performed, at each return, by my native weather,

For burial of the closing distances.
The scale grows less. I see the mountains near
My home at each return, dwindle and wither
The imagined woods as death to birth advances.

II

Mr Ellis, the owner of the Orange Grove
Hotel, in the suburbs of my native city,
Going after Lobengula's buried ivory,
Could never discover its guarded alcove.

Though the aasvogel and the lion's head
He took back, to stuff in the sockets of their eyes
Imitation anger with glass irises,
Might have delighted with novelty the dead

Man sewn in the skin of two oxen. Lobengula,
Whose continent has no memory, a sleeping
Moody appeasable spirit, is keeping
A long silence and two waggons of ivory.

As over the Limpopo and Magaliesberg
To the Fish River, on each Dingaan's Day,
Lifts a tinkle of drums for the broken assegai,
For the tribes broken in Johannesburg;

Lobengula's body by the river M'Lindi
Dries, and with the bones of Mziligazi, Rhodes
Lies royal, Ulodzi, upon the Matopos,
Romantic emperor and parish Alexander

Keeping his diamond in his cheek; Oom Paul
Rests in Pretoria, the Bible to a thumb
Acquainted with labour, and the premier waggon
Spanning liberty over the Orange and the Vaal;

By the banks of Umgusa, the Orange Grove
Hotel proprietor on a final safari
Approaches the tribute the last Matabele,
Lobengula, exacted with terror and love.

III

My grandfather was an elegant gentleman
Who trod behind an ox-waggon's wheels in his youth
Four hundred miles to Kimberley from Port Elizabeth,
To resuscitate the family fortune.

His love affair with money lasted a long time.
In my childhood I best remember
His glass-panelled car and European chauffeur,
And dignity in a cricket pavilion;

Or when in gardens imitating England
He in a morning-coat between two ladies
Walked. I was afraid to recognize
My father's father, and kept my distance.

Nothing became my grandfather so much as his age.
Impoverished and living in a single room,
He kept his grace and distinguished costume,
Imposing on distress and unstooping carriage.

The lady left him, but he took his congé
Like a gentleman. The old colonial
Never allowed a merely personal
Regret pour a poison in the ear of memory.

IV

My favourite myth was the legend of Dr Livingstone
With linen, salvation, beads and love in his hand,
Searching the continent for Herodotus' fountains,
And leaving after his death his heart and his guts behind.

The parson who recorded his defeat in dialectics
By an African wizard, going without a whip or a gun
In his hand, to the rivers and the inland lakes,
Among the savage and terrified, came to no harm.

Seeing the Zambesi roll like a leaf below
Him, and the valley of black humankind
Rise like an arm to religion and to their
Peace, the kindly and self-disciplined

Man in the end left their shackles forgotten,
Heard not any more the natural cry
Of the chained river. For more than freedom
He respected the curiosity

That once to glimpse the divided hill
Where the four sources of the Nile shape variously,
Was a last passion, and the final
Burial of his will and energy.

In which prayer dying, David Livingstone
Passed, and those whom he could not save
Carried his bones to Zanzibar and England,
But kept his heart and innards in their proper grave.

V
For Roy Campbell

My countryman, the poet, wears a Stetson;
He can count his enemies, but not his friends.
A retired soldier living in Kensington,
Who limps along the Church Street to the Swan.

Horses and bulls, the sable and impala,
Sparkle between his fingers, and a sun
That sleeps and rises from the Indian Ocean
Gongs the images of his passion.

He never loved liberty for her name,
Or wept on the disastrous ashes of Guernica,
But he fought for her where he could find her,
Knowing she was not lying in a newspaper column,

But bound, still bound in the aboriginal fall
From Eden and of Adam. His ancestors who came
Out of the eighteenth century and Scotland
Taught him to have no truck with the liberal.

Horses and bulls, the sable and impala,
Thunder between his fingers; as they run,
He hears another thunder in the sun,
Time and the sea about Tristan da Cunha.

On Himself

Abstracted by silence from the age of seven,
Deafened and penned by as black calamity
As twice to be born, I cannot without pity
Contemplate myself as an infant;

Or fail to speak of silence as a priestess
Calling to serve in the temple of a skull
Her innocent choice. It is barely possible
Not to be affected by such a distress.

Canons Ashby

County of squares and spires, in the middle of England,
    Where with companions I was used to rove,
Country containing the cedar of John Dryden,
    Cedar, in whose shadow of thunder and love
I saw those Caroline lawns, and musical
I heard, inaudible, those waters fall, fall

Triumphs and miseries, last poet of a golden
    Order, and under whose laurel I desire
To plant a leaf of bay, and by whose building
    To tune irregular strings, his stronger lyre
Plunging, a swan to alight, upon a clear
Music of language I delight to hear.

Not a hundred yards from where my substance wastes
    Nightly in London, John Dryden died on tick.
The air clouded, and in his garden gusts
    Shook the cedar tree; as I watched its branches flick
In a windy prolegomenon to autumn
While a sky marshalled engines to a storm,

I no longer heard those falling waters fall,
    Silence like Iris descended from a cloud,
And lawns grew dark, as that once musical
    Shadow of a cedar faded in the loud
Shades of thunder-cumuli on the grass,
Till we left the garden empty as it was.

On the Death of an Emperor Penguin in Regent's Park

A proletarian, unlikely bird, no monarch,
Whose northern relation, the Gare-fowl or Great Auk,
One hundred years has been extinct on these islands;
An ugly, blubber-jacketed, wingless giant
Laboriously transported from his desert of ice,
His house of hurricanes (uncomfortable birthplace!
Cold and insanitary, where ocean hardens!)
Has perished in the Zoological Gardens.
Tell, masochistic martyr, what ailed you?
Here there is care and comfort; what can have killed you?
Speak, shade! Were your keepers neglecting your welfare?
Did you lack anything purchasable with silver?
O stupid, ungrateful bird! Blubber and feather!
To die of desire for freedom and bad weather,
For the perch where you, pegged to a glacier's bitter stone
Outlast an Antarctic unending cyclone,
And watch, neither superb nor able, from below
A smashed world whirl away in stinging snow.

Moral Stories

I

On the first professional, Simonides, hangs a tale
Which says that he, at a banquet, was commissioned to sing
Verses in praise of his host for a sum agreed on.
The poet composed a panegyric; recited it all;
But its purchaser appeared dissatisfied with the thing:
The contract had been interpreted with too much freedom.

'Half of your verses are concerned with the Heavenly Pair!
Here, therefore, is half of your fee! If you require a full
Payment, make application to Castor, Pollux, and Co.
When poets waste verse on the Gods, I consider it fair
The Gods should condescend to foot their part of the bill.'
Everyone else at table agreed this ought to be so.

It seemed they enjoyed the joke. Before the poet could speak
His mind in words that he might have regretted, a butler
Appeared, to announce two strange gentlemen outside the door,
Who were knocking as if they'd been waiting there for a week,
Asking for Mr Simonides. What could be subtler?
One of them must have been Pollux, and the other, Castor.

Simonides quitted the room to see what they wanted,
But barely had he crossed the threshold, than its roof fell in,
And beams squashed the cheat like a cockroach, and everyone
    else;
The incident left the poet unhurt and enchanted.
But he saw to it that the miracle lost no force in telling,
When, later, he thought any debitor likely to welsh.

The moral of the story is, that philistines should keep
All bargains which they make with artists, and pay up at once.
That is of course perfectly obvious. Nevertheless, any
Poet can point a less evident, if not a more deep,
Moral in this business of Simonides, needing funds,
Yet paid by neither the man nor the Gods one penny.

II

I met Poetry, an old prostitute walking
Along Piccadilly, one whom no one would buy,
Just a draggletail bitch with padding for each breast –
No wonder the corner boys were gay and joking!
She'd laid on paint too thick in a colour too high,
And scuttled like a red hen deprived of its nest.

But she stopped for a word with me, one of her pimps,
Her faithful old ponce still hoping for his per cent.
When I asked, 'How's business?' she shook her leary head:
'In peacetime the boys are not so keen on the nymphs;
And I am getting a bit behind with the rent.
These days the pickings are small that fall from my bed.

'Wartime was whoretime! Never mind, cheer up, lovey;
Find me another fee like the one from New York:
They pay very nicely, the Yanks – and don't look glum.
– Or go get another girl, if you want more gravy!'
She screamed, '– you've got your good looks yet – or you could work!
Go get yourself a job licking somebody's bum!'

But out of the corner of my eye I'd seen a Rolls Royce
Purr by us with a back seat full of her old friends,
Passing, like the gent in the song, the girl they'd ruined.
They lifted a disdainful nostril at her noise,
And continued, as you might expect, to pursue their ends,
With cigars drawing, and the radio carefully tuned

To a highbrow programme. So across the gutter
We caught one another's look; and as their exhaust
Echoed outside the Ritz like a burst paper bag,
Laughed like hyenas; she, with a shaking udder,
Said, 'I was a lovely piece, when they met me first!'
And lineaments of desire lit the old hag.

III

Glaucus, a god of the sea, was once a man
Inhabiting Anthedon in the provinces;
Kept body and soul together netting fish,
Till one unlucky day on a Boeotian
And desert beach he laid, dying by inches,
Nine mackerel, constituting his day's catch.

There the grass was holy. How was he to know
It was sown by Cronus? Herdsmen steered their cattle
From that theurgic plot; and wild goats even
Kept clear of the crop a god had hoped to grow.
What Glaucus thought moribund began to scuttle,
Each fish to wriggle, until, unbelieving,

Their proprietor saw the whole haul revive,
Flap, flip, flounce, hop, slip, skip into the ocean
From which his skill and trouble elicited them.
The celestial grass had brought them back to life.
Short-witted and destined, he took a notion
To taste that grass. Thus Olympus admitted him.

Sea-gods and Nereids sprang from each sea-roller
Singing to conches, as the sky, white with gulls,
Disgusted Glaucus from that time for ever.
His hair growing green as shallows, his colour
Turned blue as out of soundings, flashing with scales:
Divinity and ocean took him over.

Further persists the inveterate fable:
Rearing, off the Italian coast, his head
To blast a prodigious paean from a shell,
Transfigured, but unabandoned by trouble,
Glaucus caught sight (because luck can leave a god)
Of young Scylla one day: an unmarried girl.

She had rejected suitors more elegant
Than a whelked sea-god; and when he tried to speak,
To tell her of his love, she had no mercy,
But, as his feet were fins, departed inland.
Glaucus was inconsolable for a week,
Then thought he would consult the great witch Circe.

To whom in Aeaea he paid a visit,
Hoping to get a charm, or occult potion.
Circe, promenading in the sacred grove
Attended by her fools, – bat, pig, marmoset,
Etcetera – saw him rise from the ocean,
And, also susceptible, fell in love.

'Why need you follow Scylla? In Aeaea I
Would lie with a sea-god,' said Helios' daughter,
A holy, extremely dangerous woman,
And fixed on Glaucus a gay and subtle eye.
But he explained his love might never alter.
He would have Scylla, virgin, young, and human.

A sea-grotto, facing the Sicilian land,
Was where lovely Scylla, naked, used to swim;
In which the goddess dropped abominable
Juices, with some appropriate curses, and
Absented herself from the repellent scene
As Scylla turned to dogs below the navel.

This conduct, inexcusable and divine,
Alienated Glaucus, who loved Scylla most
(She soon to mariners became a hazard).
The once human god continued to repine,
Visiting, yearly, the Boeotian coast,
While to Aeaea came further lovers.

A Funeral Oration

Composed at thirty, my funeral oration: Here lies
David John Murray Wright, 6′ 2″, myopic blue eyes;
Hair grey (very distinguished looking, so I am told);
Shabbily dressed as a rule; susceptible to cold;
Acquainted with what are known as the normal vices;
Perpetually short of cash; useless in a crisis;
Preferring cats, hated dogs; drank (when he could) too much;
Was deaf as a tombstone; and extremely hard to touch.
Academic achievements: B.A., Oxon (2nd class);
Poetic: the publication of one volume of verse,
Which in his thirtieth year attained him no fame at all
Except among intractable poets, and a small
Lunatic fringe congregating in Soho pubs.
He could roll himself cigarettes from discarded stubs,
Assume the first position of Yoga; sail, row, swim;
And though deaf, in church appear to be joining a hymn.
Often arrested for being without a permit,
Starved on his talents as much as he dined on his wit,
Born in a dominion to which he hoped not to go back
Since predisposed to imagine white possibly black:
His life, like his times, was appalling; his conduct odd;
He hoped to write one good line; died believing in God.

Monologue of a Deaf Man

Et lui comprit trop bien, n'ayant pas entendu.
  Tristan Corbière

It is a good plan, and began with childhood
As my fortune discovered, only to hear
How much it is necessary to have said.
Oh silence, independent of a stopped ear,
You observe birds, flying, sing with wings instead.

Then do you console yourself? You are consoled
If you are, as all are. So easy a youth
Still unconcerned with the concern of a world
Where, masked and legible, a moment of truth
Manifests what, gagged, a tongue should have told;

Still observer of vanity and courage
And of these mirror as well; that is something
More than the sound of violin to assuage
What the human being most dies of: boredom
Which makes hedgebirds clamour in their blackthorn cage.

But did the brushless fox die of eloquence?
No, but talked himself, it seems, into a tale.
The injury, dominated, is an asset;
It is there for domination, that is all.
Else what must faith do deserted by mountains?

Talk to me then, you who have so much to say,
Spectator of the human conversation,
Reader of tongues, examiner of the eye,
And detective of clues in every action,
What could a voice, if you heard it, signify?

The tone speaks less than a twitch and a grimace.
People make to depart, do not say 'Goodbye'.
Decision, indecision, drawn on every face
As if they spoke. But what do they really say?
You are not spared, either, the banalities.

In whatever condition, whole, blind, dumb,
One-legged or leprous, the human being is,
I affirm the human condition is the same,
The heart half broken in ashes and in lies,
But sustained by the immensity of the divine.

Thus I too must praise out of a quiet ear
The great creation to which I owe I am
My grief and my love. O hear me if I cry
Among the din of birds deaf to their acclaim
Involved like them in the not unhearing air.

An Invocation to the Goddess

O sea born and obscene
Venus I see ascend
Fishbright upon a shell
Out of a salty pool
Angels and flesh attend,
The dolphin-sewn and blown
Mirrors of sea surround
As bawdy as a boy
That blank desirous form.
The goddess smiles from joy,
I look her in the groin;
Her seakale coloured eyes
Acknowledge her concern.
Not the ideal but real
Half sheltered by her hand,
Sty of ambiguities
Offensive and divine.
Venus preferring joy
Defenceless from the sea
Attending to defend,
Feminine, debonair,
Step naked to the shore.
Step, wound in your hair,
And singing galleries
Fish, fowl, flesh, surround you.
I cry your worshipper
Upon this island ground
Down by a sky and still
Crying borne by a sea,
Rejected and acclaimed.
Announce perfection, smile
Upon what is deformed,
Accept what is, and be.

Adam at Evening

The falling sun stands on a hill
And shall for quarter of an hour
Before I see the darkness come
To lapse for us the labouring farm.
The long shafts range (against the night
To which a half-lost globe conforms)
As, once, before the Eden gate,
Those hostile and obedient arms.

In the garden where I was made
Ran through the original grass
The alert novelties, hoofed or pawed,
Unprofitable and harmless.
There was nothing to use or fear,
All things existed in their praise.
Each bird its phoenix broke the air,
And fiery imagos flew and strummed.

Last of the inaugural park,
Last bestowed, fatally endowed
The Friday that the spirit breathed
Choice to the dust of his image,
Between the dumb and bursting trees
The singing speechless birds and beasts,
Able to name and half to create
I walked articulate and proud.

The leaflit concepts moved between
The minted light and primal shade
As the first things for the first time
Obeyed their delight and obeyed
The nature that had created them.
A blackbird on a thornless thorn
Whistled to its marvellous world,
A world where nothing had been born.

The pomegranate to my hand
Bowed, and a berry from its spray.
To all things I returned a name:
Substantives hovering to my tongue
Became them. They in turn became
More than they were. Fish, water, bees,
The dolphin antelopes that leapt,
Or moon and stars as they came out,

Existed also as my poem.
Was a spiritual pride
Conceived in this creating hour,
That, rearing at the flanks of Eve,
As a scotched angel spoke to her?
Then the gambler lost his throw,
Then the consequence began
That cannot be ended now.

The smoulder of a grounded sun
Burns under conglomerate shade,
Invites the falling dark to fall
Which, smoking from a bloodless east,
Blots out my stead. Goodbye the light,
Let darkness shelter man and beast.
The valley fills its pool with night.
My children sleep below the hill.

Rhapsody of a Middle-aged Man

These are the middle years, and I attend
Experience and the dying of the heart.
I don't feel melancholy. The idea of an end
To the world that I am cheers me up.
Only I used to feel, before, what now I know.
Enjoying more, I care for less and less,
And cherish what I do not understand –
The gaiety at the heart of mysteries.

What astonishes most is to look back and find
That there is really nothing to regret.
O my lost despairs! Where, where have you died?
Why did you go away and send me no report?
I see there is achievement in a leaf
Because it broke the bud, courage in a wall
Because it stands; a beatitude in grief
– Committed as I am to the absurd.

How can I take the universe as solemn
Seeing it's prodigal, wastes and spends,
Has no concern with thrift or responsibility
Any more that a hero with a roll of fivers
On a Saturday night taking care of his friends.
The unselective benevolence is disquieting.
What about tomorrow and the final reckoning?
He won't worry, he's the final reckoning.

As one grows older one gets caught up more
In the precipitate irresponsible gaiety.
I ought to spare time to consider the bomb
And the likelihood of no future for humanity.
But spring comes along, and trees burst into banknotes,
Or I am observing the delicate limbs of a fly
Sampling a lump of sugar on a café table.
The singing nightingales had no time for Agamemnon.

There are no consolations, none are required.
The fury and despair are the vanity.
I see the exhilaration of the numinous
Regard the tears we shed with a dry eye.
Alas, what happened? Am I no longer sensitive?
What took my tragic gown and crown away?
What leaves me standing like a fool in the huge
Gale of the universe, naked to joy?

The godhead is in the instant of being,
The Niagara of our squandered time
Sculpting its form in the movement of its falling.
No one drop more precious than the others gone
Looking for the matches, making love or a poem,
Waiting for the bus or an old age pension.
I am not called to balance such accounts or fear
Whether the waste is worth the prospect I admire.

Still one ought to end on the serious note.
I can see a number of attitudes to strike.
The trouble is they seem fundamentally comic.
And, when one thinks, it is easier to invest
In lacrimae rerum. You get a good dividend.
But how can I pull the heartstrings of a harp
I can no longer use in the ironic midday.
When he came out of hell what tune did Orpheus play,
Was it delight or frenzy that tore his bones apart?

At a Café Table

Sitting at a café table
Under Lucullus' garden
I saw the fountain fall
And the volatile playing
Of beneficent water
Subsist no less than stone
Or marble statuary
As a perpetual form

Yet transient as today.
Trolleys with antennae
Clinging to overhead wires
And stuttering Lambrettas
Swung by the hieroglyphic
Obelisk in the square;
Rapt under a portico
A tourist consulted a guide;

Established upon the real
Rose of the perpetual
The ephemeral city smiled.
Beyond the frontier they
Assembled apocalypse.
Upon the Palatine
The eighteenth-century garden,
Formally casual,

Overlaid with elegant sadness
Cypress, columnar pine,
Those Caesarian houses
And grandiose débris.
Calm on the Capitoline,
Over the roofs of Rome,
Over a bridled stallion,
Aurelius stretched an arm

Blessing the Roman idea.
Beyond the frontier they
Prepared apocalypse –
I watched the fountain play
And vanishing water
Survive no less than stone;
Ephemeral succession
Subsume eternal form.

A Visit to the Protestant Cemetery

First we discovered the pyramid. It looked famous,
The tomb of a Roman Vanderbilt or Astor.
So many tombs in the city – Augustus,
Saint Peter, Hadrian, Saint Cecilia,
And, eminently unremembered, Cestius.
We were tourists having a look at the grave of Keats
In the burial-ground of the exiled and heretic.
Their marble gleamed like ectoplasm. Cypresses
Maintained correctly a hypnotic kind of beauty,
And having induced, adorned melancholia.
We read the wild epitaphs of the nineteenth century
(That is, the English ones: some were Russian or Greek)
Lamenting exile, eulogizing the departed,
Perpetuating immemorabilia
With an abandon and assurance which
I have learned to envy even if I do not admire.
Having seen what was expected of us (two tombs)
And an excavated site near by (habitation of cats
Who owned themselves, and it; they looked a bit lean,
And slightly mad, I thought) I shut Baedeker.
'It's time we went back to the car.' 'Who feeds those cats?'
'A society has been organized for their care.'

By the Effigy of St Cecilia

Having peculiar reverence for this creature
Of the numinous imagination, I am come
To visit her church and stand before the altar
Where her image, hewn in pathetic stone,
Exhibits the handiwork of her executioner.

There are the axemarks. Outside, in the courtyard,
In shabby habit, an Italian nun
Came up and spoke: I had to answer, 'Sordo.'
She said she was a teacher of deaf children
And had experience of my disorder.

And I have had experience of her order,
Interpenetrating chords and marshalled sound;
Often I loved to listen to the organ's
Harmonious and concordant interpretation
Of what is due from us to the creation.

But it was taken from me in my childhood
And those graduated pipes turned into stone.
Now, having travelled a long way through silence,
Within the church in Trastevere I stand
A pilgrim to the patron saint of music

And am abashed by the presence of this nun
Beside the embodiment of that legendary
Virgin whose music and whose martyrdom
Is special to this place: by her reality.
She is a reminder of practical kindness,

The care it takes to draw speech from the dumb
Or pierce with sense the carapace of deafness;
And so, of the plain humility of the ethos
That constructed, also, this elaborate room
To pray for bread in; they are not contradictory.

Campo Santo

I was adolescent when last in Genoa.
All that I now have to look back on was before me:
Twenty-eight years of doing nothing, growing older,
And a few verses, not good enough, and not many.

History, also – events that disturb newspapers.
I read of the bombardment. The ruins say it was real.
Yet these children deny it, these promenaders and cigarette-
    salesmen;
And they're right, history doesn't happen, it's what we feel

Inside us that really happens, and we feel very little
In the event, after all; a large frivolity
Of natural existence circumscribing the human soul
As if our father, which art in heaven, had taken pity.

But does one change? No, one finds oneself. I revisit,
Catching a filobus opposite a trattoria chianti-hung,
A past sensation (as I believe is the middle-aged habit):
The great cemetery of Genoa that I visited when I was young.

Seraphim, urns, obelisks, headstones and junk advancing
Consolidate positions on its spectacular hill:
The heart rises to see the battleflags of oblivion
Among municipal cypresses and yellow gravel!

The merchants, the widows, the children, the shop-assistants,
Brothers and sisters in Christ, the political heroes,
The tenants of furnished flats, and opera-singers,
An army of anonyms established upon the glacis!

It is absurd to be human? Here is the gallery
Where a lost epoch celebrates in exact stone
A bourgeois flowering and perpetuates its regalia
Of 1880 to the last waistcoat-button.

I am impressed, now as then, by a rococo energy,
The impeccably respectable déjeuner sur l'herbe
Effect that is gained by each Sunday-suited effigy,
Marble hat in marble hand, juxtaposed with superb

Negligently half-naked breasts (an angel's or a grief's)
Which would seem to offer practical consolation:
What it is to have the courage of bad taste!
The uninhibited inhibitions have their eloquence.

Here was I then, en l'an quatorzième de mon âge,
Stepped out of a liner en route from Africa,
To experience these very recognitions, admire
That stone friar pray with a twig of mimosa in his ear.

So much seen, so many countries, since I was here last.
How remarkable after so much education,
All those involvements with so many men and women,
To find one is fundamentally the same person

As at the start of the long journey to nowhere or
Here and now. The dust is a bit thicker on the tombs.
The self is not altered. One is the discoverer
Of oneself, not the world. As the babe that issues from

The womb might have told us. Here in the Campo Santo
At Staglieno near Genoa, where first I landed
In Europe and Italy twenty-eight years ago,
What do I know but myself I begin to know?

As the still-questioning attest with these monuments,
Many questions have been settled in this holy field:
Whether for the adolescent, prisoner of opinions,
Or the man, captive to the bow and spear of experience.

Kleomedes

Both Plutarch and Pausanias tell a story
That is a worry to imagination.
It's of the athlete Kleomedes, a moody
Instrument for a theophanic anger
And for an outrageous justice not our own.

Plutarch reports the tale in the barest outline,
Evidently having no comment to offer,
And certainly no word of explanation
To throw light upon what happened to Kleomedes
Or the subsequent oracular non sequitur.

As for Kleomedes: at the Olympic Games he
Killed his opponent in the boxing-contest.
The ox-felling blow was not his, he claimed; the
Fury struck through him, it was not his own strength.
He'd won, but they withheld the palm nevertheless.

The injustice of it. Nursing rage like a pot-plant,
Watering it with his thoughts, which were few and stupid,
When he drank with others he drank with his back turned
To cherish that shrub till one more bud had sprouted.
It was growing to be a beauty and he loved it.

The palm of victory, his by rights, denied him.
Well, he would go home to Astypalaea.
There they would understand; were they not his own kin?
Anger. His heart fed an ulcer. Would it disappear
At sight of the headland of his own dear island?

So Kleomedes went away; his rage didn't.
It's hard being done by foreigners, but far worse
When the people one grew up with see no harm in it.
Even the light of the noonday sun seemed altered
In the familiar market-place where fools chaffered.

Wrath. Wrath. In an access of it he stood up.
May God damn the lot of you, he said, seizing the first
Thing his eye fell on: it was a marble column.
Ah, and he tugged. Tugged. And his brow pimpled with sweat.
Possessed, he exerted more than his might. It tumbled.

Slowly a coping-stone slid. Then the whole roof
Collapsed with a roar. Thunder. A pall of dust
Stood like a rose where had been a schoolroom of children.
Kleomedes saw their blood lapped up by the earth.
There was silence and grief. Then a cry, Murderer!

Murderer! Murderer! He was among strangers.
Hatred and anger in that man's, that woman's eye.
And now they were one eye. The eye of an animal,
Hackles up, about to rend. Its name Mob, hairy
Gorgon. Brute, it is a beast made up of us all;

May none of us ever be or see it! He saw,
Miserable quarry, lust ripple its muscles.
Act now or die! He acted. Ran for sanctuary
To the holy temple, the temple of Pallas Athena:
Mob may respect the precinct of the armed goddess.

But what does a beast know of gods? He heard baying
Hard at his heels. Saw a chest there in the forecourt.
Prayed it be empty. He lifted the lid. Stepped in
Pulling the lid behind him, and held it fast shut.
More strength that his own held it against all efforts.

I don't understand the story from this point on.
Here enters mystery. Levering a crowbar
They heaved at hinges; the wood groaned and a hasp cracked.
Now for the fellow. Kleomedes did not appear.
They looked; but the chest was empty; the man was gone.

It was anticlimax. Fear fluttered from dismay.
They were people again. The sun continued to shine
As it had done. There were the children to bury.
Catastrophe and the violated shrine
Remained; and, before them, a vacant box grinning.

Astypalaea sent to Delphi embassies
To ask the pythoness what these events forebode;
What might be their significance; where the guilt lay.
The oracle kept silence. Then vouchsafed its word.
'The last of the heroes was Kleomedes.'

Plettenberg's Bay

Plettenberg's Bay, the year nineteen-twenty-seven,
Myself with five senses, my world a new penny,
A time and a place as halcyon as any.
I had come by way of the Garden of Eden

Which is not far from Knysna, in the forest.
Of course I thought it was the authentic garden,
Its trees the trees which shaded Eve and Adam
Before they had bartered wisdom for knowledge.

'This is it,' said the driver of the hired car
Halting beside a glade. And I heard the lulling
Fall of the water of a stream concealing
Its muscles under a ferned and shaded bower.

This was the spot visited by archangels.
Alpha and Omega in the cool of the day
Walked in that evergreen grove, his beasts at play,
As our first parents with naked genitals

Stepped unaware of their paradisiac boredom
Or of the burden of their frivolous choice.
Why not? The African quality of the place,
Of seeming at once new created and pristine,

The clarity of its light, and depth of its shade,
Would probably convince me, could I return,
This was the site of the original Eden,
Though I looked at it with the eyes of middle age.

I was then aged seven; but I remember still
After a quarter century, the quarter hour
I spent in a green and flowerless clearing where
I heard silence itself, immense and arboreal,

Listening to a hidden stream which defined it
With noise, the shock and fall of water on stone.
Then I could not know what for so long I have known,
That it was an Eden which I inhabited

In my young age, wheresoever I might be;
That already my departure was preparing.
Later I'd look back on my holidaying
And innocent unconsciousness of intense joy

At neighbouring Plettenberg's Bay, where the ocean
Pitched into the beaches its pounding cavalry's
Implacably cantering pennants of water,
As a farewell party, given by that garden.

My father fishing from the cliffs above the sea:
Far out he hurls his line; I hear it hiss and swoop;
As I watch it fall, think I hear (but can't) the slap
Of the sinker as it hits the water far below.

Or I am bending over transparent shallows
Where small fish swim and flowerlike sea-urchins bloom,
And there are volutes and conches; but each is a home
– Hermit-crabs inhabit the desirable shells.

The voices of children are light upon the sand
Where the wave posting letters of pebble and weed
With a destroying sigh wheels back to its huge bed
And winds in its rumour all the noises of the land.

When, later, visited by unbudging deafness
– That accident I turned into a destiny –
I saw all movement vibrate fantastically
Till I could not hear my silence for its loudness

Except when everything was completely still,
And not a leaf moved aeolian to the wind,
I comprehended how no power could suspend
Or obscure the faithful vision that all is well

Invested in me then, when the commonplaces
Wore a miraculous bloom of new creation,
All visible things invested with affection.
I am not speaking of what merely solaces.

The sacred pair at their exit from the garden
Hid with garlands the place of generation.
Henceforward suffering may be their condition,
The world a wilderness they are to labour in:

But they did not lose the knowledge that they could not lose
That conviction watered by aboriginal streams
And to be watered now by tears of human kind
– In the desert of loss as unlikely as a rose

Declaring desolation to be a mirage –
That unreasonable conviction of a good
In the face of the evidence of vicissitude,
Infelicity, hatred, old age and outrage!

On the Margin

I

What I like about art, and what you might call nature,
Is, in the last resort, their absolute absence of
Adumbration of information, propaganda,
Of even, *pace* the romantics, moral uplift.

A tree or a mountain is there, being itself,
Not responsible for emotions of the beholder
Or whether a shift of light, moonrise or rain falling
Should make him feel good, resolve at least to do better.

Their inveterate superfluity lets them speak
As do paintings, carvings, and the collocation
Of words or noise or both (i.e. poetry, music)
On matters about which there is no communication.

Love, death, liberty, and what we are all here for,
Whether the date is November twenty-three or doomsday,
Discussions of this kind, they somehow manage to ignore:
Theirs is a message of purest frivolity.

Affirming the unprovable, they have nothing to say
But that the fine point of existence, the instant's span
Between the void before and the void after, is really
Valid (and what is the use of knowing this?). Again

They do not say anything but by analogy.
Ulysses deriding Polyphemus, the play of Hamlet,
Bach's Italian concerto, a bird or the sea,
Reflect the unbelievable; which is a kind of joy.

II

Nostalgia and sentimentality are perhaps all
That incline me (which includes you also) to determine
The former attributes of the world, noted in childhood,
To have been immutability and a, well, pristine

Anteriority – things appearing ancient and novel:
Having existed from time's beginning, like water and air,
Yet original because encountered by a young
Eye; to whom a rock is old and new as a motor-car.

Now and eternity were then scarcely disparate things.
The universe remained a stasis, and without future
Because one had so little experience of a past;
The present, an incomparable gift, was for ever.

Yesterday as valid as today, with the sun's rising
Due at morning; the weather of noon; light fades, to return
After a procession of stars, with a moon sometimes;
Days recreating themselves, not coming in succession.

So, without memory or apprehension, the animal
Eye of a child takes in the innocence of the whole
Arrangement, it is all for his benefit, therefore good;
His fraction of being, of light and air, short but eternal.

III

Here I was interrupted. What took me to Inniskeen
In Monaghan, Ireland, a foggy day in December,
To watch a strange soil, glaucous and stony, fall in spadefuls
When the priest had done, on the yellow lid of a coffin?

Candles fluttered in the hands of acolytes, a few rooks
Flapped over their rookery, a crowd as black as they were
Stood silently, saw the grave fill, heard the spades tamp and
    shape
A mound as long as a man, a native of that place.

How should I not pay my respects to an honourer of
The ordinary and mundane, who would transfigure
A canal bank seat, a stick floating on the water, or
A hospital washbasin, with his attention of love?

The ephemeral is immortal, and vice versa.
The universe is particular, we have here and now
But nothing else whatever. Yet I see his grave take shape
And, appropriate beyond my understanding, his taciturn

Resumption by locality elevates the spirit.
'R.I.P. Patrick Kavanagh, died 1967.'
We do not know why it was thought right or for whose sake
The hearse halted at Pembroke Road, and the farm where he was born.

IV

I have to thank you, for I may as well thank somebody:
Adam's god suits my unmathematical imagination.
We will land on the moon any moment, to find you gone,
Dodged behind a new smokescreen – quasars or anti-matter.

Another Bishop of Woolwich will bring you up to date:
A concept of god, palatable to human reason,
Will always be in demand. Which doesn't bother you, I suppose.
You have a price for sparrows and see that we pay it:

We are not without use, from the point of view of sparrows.
It takes, perhaps, as much trouble to create a molecule
And the laws it lives by, as an antelope or Sirius;
Thine is the abundance, the wastefulness, and the energy.

It is through imagination god can communicate
Whether as moral concept, virgin-born, or thunderer.
His the misery and mistake; burning; I could do better
(As who could not) yet not conceive his altitudes of delight.

V

They are not like us, we are like them: I mean animals.
Which of us has not been a fish, at least in the womb?
Whose passions we share (even our politics derive from theirs)
But who have no language; the present is enough for them.

They cannot regret the past, fear the future, or tell lies
Even to themselves. They can only communicate feelings.
It seems to me that where we have knowledge they have wisdom;
We apprehend, but they know. I wish I could be as selfish

As a bird perched on a hedge-twig or an area wall
About the purpose and function of the morning, or
The sunset promise. For the bird, no speculation;
Its wholeness is in acceptance and its faith natural.

Who cannot learn from us, but from whom we can learn something
Concerning ourselves and the imagination of god:
The latter devious, theatrical, and obscure, being
Implicit in slagheaps, a knee-joint, or a spider's web,

Crucifixions, the shape of a leaf, spermatozoa,
And wet afternoons in Leeds. While as for ourselves
We are not especially cherished, and maybe
Have no more claim to attention than phenomena.

VI

An anniversary approaches: of the birth of god
In a stable, son of a virgin and a carpenter,
But really issued from loins of omnipotent glory:
A babe, ejected from the thighs, greased in mucus and blood,

Weeping with its first breath, suffering the cold air, high king
Of the galaxies, and powerless as a fieldmouse.
Over him breathe the oxen; shepherds who have seen a star
Honour the obscure event; and, they say, three travelling

Magi, or charlatans. This is the messenger of hope;
The military have been instructed to deal with him.
A wholesale killing, their invariable strategy,
While abolishing a generation, fails of effect.

We are asked to believe all this (it's only to start with).
What a jumble of the impossible and casual,
Of commonplace mixed with violence; ordinary muddle;
The props and characters scruffy; at best unheroic.

Yet accordant with the disposition of things holy
As we understand them; whose epiphanies are banal,
Not very aesthetic; gnomic; unremarkable;
And very much like what we have to put up with daily.

VII

To get back to art. Panegyric, it celebrates
The existence of things. Remember Helen Keller
Living in a mute vague, an environment of touch,
Texture transfigured into sound, smell into colour;

Who from a disablement of perception created
Forms of the real, images valid and strange,
Interpreters of void and of silence, hinges
Between what was and what seemed. And our disabled

Apprehension needs approximations of the real
Whose figure, recreated out of true, the mind
May recognize as there and praise for being,
Its blind lineaments realized by feeling.

A Cemetery in Dumfriesshire

A town of red sandstone, built beside a river,
Where stands my grandfather's house, now a dogs' home.
Each time I come, I meet the same kind of weather:
Gusty, wet, melancholy, smelling of autumn.
The spring was my grandfather's favourite season.

Depending, like most of us now, on no real place,
I like to think, here is somewhere I partly come from.
A particularity, though undistinguished.
A bridge, a river bank, and a high street known
To my people, emigrant or long underground.

Here their Scottish headstones in a graveyard achieve
Articulate pomp, where death is celebrated
Properly, with enjoyment. None of them are left.
I remember the last, an old man who waited
Alone in a big house, among parcels labelled

Ready for dispatch, like himself. Here is his name
Where he looked forward to having it, set beside
An older lettering; both now weathered the same.
That cross he raised for her was imaginative
But his grief may have been romantic, like her tomb.

Constricted and focused by a locality,
The lives appear complete; were at least completed
Within a definite frame, not of place only.
And despite hopes and purposes defeated,
I think it is their relevance I envy.

Chester Car Park

Just to put it on record that for the month of May
I was living at Chester, parked by the river Dee,
In an old blue caravan under a hawthorn tree.

Grosvenor Bridge spanned the river, flying high,
And hid the racecourse from view. The gasworks and railway,
A wood coming down to the water with cow-parsley

Brushing its knees, were likewise screened from my eye.
But I'd see the salmon-fishers returning early,
Rowing a haul of wet meshes home before the day;

A pair of swans reflect beside the cemetery
On the farther bank, sheltered by yew and holly;
And a seagull fishing at dusk when light was pearly.

I was placed fortunately, if accidentally,
To watch the traditional progress of primavera
On a patch of ground go by pastorally.

The hawthorn was dense with white petals till greenery
Broke through, balding it with a variant of glory;
Various birds explained that the world is an aviary.

But June burst in weeping, and left the door open. Windy
And wet the summer. And though now the show is over,
I had a good time; I can say that sincerely.

The Lakes

How probable to the eye, this collation
Of miniature wilderness, delicious lakes,
Where low-slung clouds lift eminences higher,
Hiding the apexes with vaporous flanks.

Aspects of water – cataract, stream, and cloud,
Lake, mist and river, modulate with stone
In all its forms – rock, boulder, scree, and crag –
To entertain and serve imagination.

Light converses between the fixed and shifting:
Cloudraker hills, the streams that lance and fade;
Each valley aerial in a vague refraction
Imposed upon the bosom of its lake.

Beyond them and behind, there where unbothered
Still pools look skyward, each a single eye,
Solitude like a wildflower to be gathered
Waits for the cursory footstep patiently.

How understandable to have apprehended
Nature and the God of nature on our side.
A valley counterpoints a mountain cadence;
A lovely sheet of water lies quiet;

And washed in evening, when light is clearest,
The panorama, thoroughly admired,
Glances at its reflection in the water
Like a young girl successfully attired.

Grasmere Sonnets

In a tea-garden overhanging Rotha
On whose clear surface cardboard packages
And other discards take their voyages
To the quiet lake, I wondered what he'd say,
Old mountain-trotter with a nose like Skiddaw
Safely asleep there where the river nudges
Its Coca-Cola can into the sedges,
Were his bleak eye to brood upon our day.
Exultant at the goings-on of nature,
Eavesdropping winds' and waters' talk,
That tough egoist, bathetic as ever,
Overlooks at Town End a macadam car park,
Folkweave booths, postcards, and suburbia,
The desert of our century; he'll not baulk.

He was always fortunate and was given
An enviable present; which he employed
To provide the inanimate with a voice,
A mountain stream giving a tongue to a mountain.
For he said that they haunted him like passion,
The air, earth, and water, and light and clouds,
With which he would intelligibly rejoice,
At one with their solitary interaction.
But his present is past and has for audience
A torn paper floating on the water,
A smell of tar and coaches: a technological present
Of bodily comfort and abominable fear,
Of no resolution and no independence;
Yet never think that he is not with us here.

The mountain winds pummel Fairfield and Helvellyn,
Scrubbing the hills with a blanket of vapour.
Recognize there the inimical nature
Of those elements beyond our controlling
If any are. Call it a foretelling
Of our victorious and rational slaughter
Of useless creation: his versing nostalgia
For the other lives that we see disappearing.
Let him lie there by Rotha without remark.
Hiding and half disclosing, the veils of rain
Make a Chinese painting of his ashen lake,
Of the slopes where woods deciduously mourn
Another autumn about to overtake
A summer's progress with a bony arm.

There is a cragbound solitary quarter
Hawk's kingdom once, a pass with a tarn
High on its shoulder. Inscribed on a stone
With graveyard letters, a verse to his brother
Says it was here they parted from each other
Where the long difficult track winding down
A bald blank bowl of the hills may be seen
Leading the eye to a distant gleam of water.
After that last goodbye and shake of the hand
A bright imagination flashed and ended;
The one would live on, for forty years becalmed
Among the presences he had commanded –
Those energies in which the other foundered,
Devoured by wind and sea in sight of land.

The Deviser

With what extraordinary delights he
Informs his creation – what madness is in
His ideas for vegetable propagation!
That remarkable arrangement between a bee

And a rose would not occur to an engineer.
To me a rose looks beautiful, but I imagine
It is desirable merely to the busy one
Up to his honeybags in a petal vagina.

A rose is no good to me except to look at.
Between the human legs there is a crop of hair
Which I find delectable but cannot admire
Merely, as in the case of a rose, in the abstract.

Like the insect, I too have my honeypot,
One that it would not occur to me to devise
With such thrift, considering the various
Other uses to which it is put,

Some of which I have no taste for. But I suppose
He is not going to let us forget we came from
The dirt he shaped his image of, if Adam
Was his image and not the world that is.

All the same one has to admit the set-up is odd.
After making every allowance for his delight
I do not understand why joy should permeate
All his devices and each expedient.

Words

Often, when I go walking,
And the dialogue resumes, the
Interior gossip which has been
Going on since identity,

I've wished to put in a poem
Those illuminations, percepts
– What percepts! But in this art one may
Only be spoken through, although

At the same time I am saying
What only I can say. Older
Than we are, words and the language
Select our valid obsessions.

Constructing from words the poem,
I say what they say I should say
Rather than what I would say. They
Use us where we would use them.

The syntactical artefact
Implicit in its material
Like sculpture. Thus like a sculptor
One obeys the wood or marble

And, while shaping, collaborates
With a form that desires itself:
Till the unlooked-for for which one
Looked for asserts a perfection.

Words, language: they have their eyes on
The unborn. Their order proceeds
From the dead but not yet done with.
Thus, when I fiddle with them, I

Meddle with matter existing
In other, further dimensions.
The poet is detached from the poem
With which he had something to do.

Swift

A peculiar dropout, a small fledgeling swift,
Stayed with us for a while as a kind of guest.
Voracious, he sat on his belly all day
Squeaking as high as a bat, except when fed.

Streamlined for flight, yet too topheavy to fly
Or take to the air in which he was meant to live,
How might he leave the ground, though designed for the sky?
Happy to squeak and eat, he made no attempt.

Feet like talons, powerful to cling and grip,
The hooded greedy face of a predator,
He gobbled his meat like a dragon, remained fat,
Satisfied and demanding, until one day

The scimitar wings for no reason suddenly
Beat ten times to the second. He upended
Himself with furious flutters; keeled half over
Battering with black feathers at the level

Tabletop he'd been squatting on, and almost
Stood on his head. Nothing would keep him quiet.
Having made clear to us that his time had come
He was ready to go, our pensioner of a fortnight.

We fetched him out to a field, carried in the palm
Of a hand; bowled the soft body like a ball
Into the air, which received him falling, but
His wings found their element, then scissoring

With panic sleight, bore the surprised and able
Creature to his inheritance; who sank,
Lifted and sank, with fear and confidence
Exulting into the distance, out of our sight.

Rook

I

Tumbling across a field like a hat blown off
He made for the rookery – run, stumble, flap,
Flap, flap; but as I gained on him gave up

Suddenly, and lay calm with confident eye,
Anaesthetized for death. Sentimentality!
I should have left him for a fox's dinner.

Began a posthumous life for this rook
Whose dead wing – broken, perhaps, by a gunshot –
Dragged buckled feathers, grounding him for good.

Yet not quite. With admirable jealous
Obdurateness, arrogant to stay alive,
He adapted to his luck; learned to manage

That hobbled, unbalanced limb; to climb a ladder
Hop, hop, up to the porch-eaves, or unsteadier
Branches of a garden tree: comic endeavour!

Independent, indomitable, therefore clown,
Obstinate in endurance on one wing,
Stuck to a bough though wind must blow him down.

II

Salvaged by us, nursed, partly tamed, here sheltering,
A rook with four white feathers and a broken wing.
He ought to be put down, he will never again fly;
Death would be better for the bird, logically.
Nature was arranging it: starvation or a fox.
The write-off could have served a practical purpose
Fertilizing a field, or in something's stomach
Subsuming further life. The crippled rook
Cannot forage; we furnish him water and food.
Our sentimental intelligence interfered

With his dispatch, created a pensioner
No use to himself or us, except to flatter
Our charity. A monster, a posthumous bird:
If the world were perfect he would now be dead.

In this aberration of the natural order
The rook bears some guilt. He is collaborator
With those who wrongly keep him alive. He could go,
Find his own death. He is not captive. But no,
Though never to take the air he means to live,
This hobble-wing, bright eye, black-purple plumage,
Intently selfish, determined against pity.

E.P. at Westminster

Old whitebearded figure outside the abbey,
Erect, creating his own solitude,
Regards, tremulously, an undistinguished crowd,
Literati of the twentieth century.
They have come to pay homage to his contemporary;
He, to a confederate poet who is dead.
The service is over. Fierce and gentle in his pride,
A lume spento, senex from America,

He can only remember, stand, and wonder.
His justice is not for us. The solitary
Old man has made his gesture. Question now
Whom did the demoded Muse most honour
When she assigned with eternal irony
An order of merit and a cage at Pisa?

On a Friend Dying

I should speak in the past tense
But do not, for it seems
What was has an existence,
If only of images.

Remains a scene as still
As water, as fragile,
Floating a ghostly
Reflection. Immobile

Summer of long late-lit
Evenings in a dingy street.
A swung glow of the Marquis
Door seen from Rathbone Place.

And there remains a large room full of flowers
   Imaged on canvases, the real ones still in the garden,
And books and objects I've known for thirty years.
   Unknown to me I am taking a final leave of them

And the woman no longer young but more beautiful
   Than the young girl had been, who held all these together.
Yet that web woven over so long shall not unravel,
   Though the lives and bonds disperse like the furniture

To disassociation. Eternity, when one thinks of it,
   Exists in what has been, there residing.
In what's done and can't be changed is immortality,
   Though I may not be long remembering.

The summer of pilotless planes,
Of searchlit nights and soft,
When once upon a scare
Together we ran out

Into the naked garden
High over Archway, and
The warm leaves of laurel
Trembled in no wind.

Larger in death, mythical, those figures,
Yankel Adler, David Archer, Colquhoun and MacBryde;
Not failed gods, because our gods were failures
Standing in broken shoes with half-pints of Scotch ale.
Now would I say that it is nine o'clock at the Wheatsheaf,
That it will not be long before the place is full.

Who was it who said
Friends are born, not made?

I remember, as now
You no longer do,

The recognition
Across a long room;

After the eyes met
Was articulate

Before we had spoken
What had always been.

Julian Orde Abercrombie, 1917-1974

A Peripatetic Letter to Isabella Fey

November 1973

Dear Isabella,
              Thank you for
That card from Israel, where you are;
I am at Preston, in a train,
Travelling south to catch a plane,
And looking out of the window
At broken roofs and glass below,
Parked cars and rubble; clean and bald
New offices of a starker world
Than

  – Just as I was writing, 'Than',
The diesel drew in to Wigan,
Whose red Victorian bricks are there,
Spire, factory, and gas-holder;
And, looming in the east, a spine
Of gloomy hills, the long Pennine
Below a dirty pewter sky.

– We've pulled in and pulled out of Crewe;
Now squared-off Cheshire fields lie green,
Trees burn from ochre into dun,
Or, stripped, stand like a map of veins
Above flat fields in hedgerow lines;
And a brook, placid as a snake,
Winds flatly by the railway track
With here and there a red-brick farm,
A march of pylons, a Dutch barn;
Already we're in Staffordshire,
The Midlands; London can't be far.

I love the North, and all England,
But best, perhaps, a vanished land:
The one I had a glimpse of, when
Between the Severn and the Nen
From '34 to '42

I spent those summers long ago
Without a notion that so much –
Things common as a hedge or ditch,
A line of mowers scything hay,
A stook of corn, etcetera,
Or, running late to Cheltenham,
A long white smoke-plume slowly drawn,
The branch-line train from Honeybourne –
Was scarcely to be seen again.

January 1974

This was as far as I had got
One winter day, November 8,
Two months ago, while on the way
From Cumberland to Africa.
For when the London suburbs ran
To meet me, I laid down my pen
(That is, I closed the typewriter),
To watch grimy, and grimier,
Victorian backyard plots flit by,
Then cuttings, until, quietly,
The engine halted at Euston.

Twenty-four hours of London,
The peculiar bit I love and know
(That dingy littoral of Soho
– Now pasture where dinosaur heads
Of power-shovels dip and feed –)
Then, full of grief and Guinness, I
Boarded a plane to Italy:
From whence, from Rome, a jumbo-jet
Carried me southwards through the night
And further from the ego who
Began, but could not continue,
As he approached his other home
And other self, his letter-poem.

What had brought me flying over
To Africa was my mother,
Living in, and older than,
Johannesburg, where I was born;
Eternal, maternal love
Returning me to Orange Grove.

How recreate the glassed-in stoep
Where my bed was, four floors up,
That overlooked a bioscope,
A golf-course, and Voortrekkershoogte
(One of the hills whose thin blue line
Edges the horizon like a stain),
And the green tree-tops which hid
Corrugated iron red
Roofs of Norwood bungalows?
Or, when the sun dropped below,
Slid like a penny in its slot
Under the highveld's rim, and brought
The white stars out, and the white moon,
And the Lido Café's neon,
Revive those moments of being
In a familiar, alien
Environment, which absence from
Underscores, at each return,
After half a life elsewhere,
That will or nill my roots are there?

Still living there, my mother, born
In Dumfriesshire in '81
When klipspringers used to haunt
The kopjes of Witwatersrand;
Born when that glass and concrete flower
Of Langlaagte and cheap labour,
Those withered hills of yellow spoil,
The Jameson Raid, and Treason Trial,
The fractured lives, and fractured hearts,
Lay implicit in the quartz.
It's strange that everything around,
Crumbling suburban mansions, drowned

In their own gardens, under tall
Oaks already memorial
To a way of life half gone,
That all things there I look upon,
Growth or artefact, should be
Younger than her living eye.

A spacious view, and full of clouds,
At evening, from her high windows:
Below, above the summer green,
There's a blue smoke of blossoming
Jacaranda through the tree-tops threading;
Vague curtains of unfallen rain.
I watch her blue and fading eyes
Look inward, reminisce;
Histories not of this land.

She talks to me of Henry Lamb,
A wicked wit, a wicked eye,
A Strachey portrait still half-dry;
Of a tide flooding Solway sand,
Two children running hand in hand –
Their deliverer, unknown.
'My father gave him half-a-crown.'
Like that sea long ago, the dark
Wells up below Magaliesberg,
And washes over veld and trees.
'He never showed affection to us,
And so I never got enough,'
She says, who gave me too much love.
Then back to Henry Lamb again.

And were there not the mornings when
Like a Jo'bourgeois, bright and early,
I'd catch a doubledecker trolley
(City-Stad), pull up the hill,
Pass the cracked cement of Yeoville,
Look for St John's low red-brown tower
Remembering those lost and other
Selves that time and change have killed,

The man, the schoolboy, and the child,
Who saw the same yet not the same
Prospects; for and because of whom
These constructs, mediocre, tatty,
Possess, as now I concede, beauty.
Though outside the O.K. Bazaar
The mutilated, as before,
Are squatting, patient, black, and humble,
I miss the Pioneer Hotel,
Ornate and pinchbeck and decayed;
The glassed, voluminous Arcade's
Overblown and plaintive
Grandiosity of 1890.
Most of the old stuff's coming down;
You'd not think, in so new a town,
The current fashion to erase
Could so affect the sense of place,
And as in London or Paris,
Effacing more than history,
Erect the outworks of Nowhere
Here, there, and everywhere.

But I best of all remember
A green summery December
Afternoon, when from the shade
Of the old Pretoria road
We turned off, where a painted sign
As in my boyhood, read: IRENE.
I'd often passed it as a boy,
But that was in the general's day.
The once I saw the general,
He was driving down the Mall,
Apple cheeks, white dagger beard,
At the Victory Parade.
No great tactician, so they say,
No De Wet, no De La Rey;
Yet his commando took the war
From Stormberg to Concordia;
Smuts for my generation was
Take or leave it, the Ou'Baas.

Along side-roads, no longer tar,
But blood-rust dirt of Africa,
We sought the old dead general's farm
Hedged and edged with heavy green
Huge eucalypti towering
Over fields where browsed oxen,
Patriarchic, biblical
As Exodus or Samuel;
And found, down in a wooded hollow,
His tin-walled, tin-roofed bungalow
Grateful for bougainvillea and
Grassblades that pricked through the red sand,
Tall trees above, a vlei below.

The whole anachronism so
Irrelevant as to be a dream,
To be the Africa we mean.

Under boulders, on a hill
Above Irene, his bones lie still;
To the north, syncretic, bland
As polythene, highrisers stand
Witness to Pretoria.
And if you look the other way
Over the water-broken highveld
Dome, you see against its rifled
And enormous monotones
The lumpy soil, and brittle bones
Of a meretricious city.

Yet to say that is too easy.
Their own history has made
Dumb ox politicians afraid,
Subverters of truth and sense,
Polyhistors of the shade of skins;
And Oppenheimer rings a bell
As Eugène Marais never will.
A consolation is, that here
Culture does not spell Career:
Between indifference and police

The real, the gay and serious
Makers would appear to thrive
Unflattered, unacademized,
Pro tem at least. There was the night
Two days before my homeward flight,
When Barney Simon took me round
To Lionel Abrahams's, and I found
With him and Nadine Gordimer
A rapport that seems seldomer
To happen, but the kind I'd know
In Fitzrovia, long ago.
And these were friends of two good men,
Of Nat Nakasa, and Bosman,
Dead men I had wished to meet,
Masters of the ironic
Throwaway, the smile that stings
Where indignation wastes in weeping.
Ill-bodied Lionel, if I
Who also am a cripple, may
So apostrophize, I see
In you a human victory:
Not a heroic, but human,
That says, 'If he can, then I can.'
I mean not only what you are
But what you did with *Renoster*.
I am not to forget your room
That held so much, shadowed and warm;
Its glass wall, where a dark garden
Looked with the moon and sadness in;
What we said, and did not say.

I sign off: desunt cetera:
And leave Johannesburg behind
And that ill country where no wind
Blows good, though it be blowing change.
Dear Isabella, I must end
This desultory and octo-
Syllabic letter to a friend.
What has been said in it is true
But of no moment; in the end

A way to record truth is to
Preserve the unimportant and
Personal, so be it moves:
The what, to find the why one loves.

Bom Jesus

On the stairway leading up to the Bom Jesus,
Shrugging along on her knees, a woman in black
Paying a penance imposed on the superstitious,
Pauses to stare. I am too polite to stare back.

I descend the hillside with one hand on a camera
And the other laid upon a balustrading.
Its eighteenth-century architect was a master,
Although his church at the top seems to lack feeling.

Effigies stare from pedestals at the valley,
Lichen has given their stone the colour of calm.
Box and rhododendron have been planted carefully
And I admire the interpolation of their green

Signatures beside the stairway. Formally mounting,
Delicately harnessing geometry to praise
The idea of order as vouchsafed to the human,
Embroidering in stone a logic of line and curve,

Parting and meeting, a minuet, its flights ascend
Through a population of apostles and sages,
At every level a fountain, on every hand
A scatter of paradises.

Below stretch the vineyards: there is a city and
A river flicking the sun's light back at my eye.
Garden of felicity, for it is a garden,
With boredom the only burden if burden it be.

But painfully crawling and praying the woman
Shuffles up to Bom Jesus. The credulous
Believe in a resurrection and in heaven.
For them the stairway has been built with a purpose.

As for me I am able to photograph it,
Enjoy its baroque fountains and seduction
Of my aesthetic sensibilities.
I have not got belief, and live in freedom.

Encounter

At Lisbon, in the Jardim Zoologico,
By the dilapidated palace where I loiter
This light and shady afternoon of October
Admiring deer, and pools, and azulejo'd

Fountains and cages – the various and quiet
Visible world, whether animate or made –
All things seem extraordinary and placid.
Fronds of jacaranda, transparent as feathers

Where seals, delighted, splash in their pond! Flamingos
Barely move, and then with the intensest grace.
There are the gazelles and Siberian tigers,
But no less strange or beautiful than these

A woman with children, like a composite flower
With children for petals. They hold her skirt and each other,
Hand in blind hand, linked figures of a frieze.
And neither they nor I admit misfortune.

They disappear, hand in hand, down the avenues
Enjoying the feel of the wind, of the sun and shadows,
And listening, as I do not, to the queer and sweet cries
Of the birds and odd beasts gathered in the garden.

Balloon
to Max and Jane

We took the children on the lake.

Wings like heartbeats, a stretched neck
Skimming over hazy water
Between an island and an island:
A wildfowl flying, black with distance.

Then a balloon, another bounty,
Hung with slung basket low above
A wooded bight, a stony bay,
Drifted like an hour hand
Across the flat and sunlit face
Of the lake, both motionless.

Yes, they will remember this;
And as I did, when young as they,
Think what is given us to see
Has always been, will always be;
Heretofore as hereafter
A duck flying, a balloon
Suspended with two people in
Its basket over Derwentwater.

The Musician

In the south aisle of the abbey at Hexham
I turned to make a remark on its Roman
Tomb; but she did not hear me, for the organ
Was playing in the loft above the rood-screen,
Laying down tones of bronze and gold, a burden
Of praise-notes, fingerings of a musician
There at the keys, a boy, his master by him,
Whose invisible sound absorbed my saying.

Music inaudible to me, barbarian.
But legible. I read in my companion
Its elation written in her elation.
'He is so young he can be only learning,
You would not have expected to hear such playing.
It's like a return to civilization.'
Unable to hear, able to imagine
Chords pondering decline, and then upwelling

There in that deliberate enclave of stone,
I remembered music was its tradition;
Its builder, Acca, taught by one Maban
To sing; who may have been the god of song,
Mabon the god of music and the young;
That another bishop of this church, St John,
Taught here a dumb man speech, says Bede; became
Patron and intercessor of deaf men.

Procession

Sober the overhead trees, and fields tilted
And framed by laborious walls on the framing hills,
No colour but a heavy green of August
Till the sun steps over a cloud, and light falls bare
On a pastoral lake and valley, where tourists
In their bright anoraks have come to stare.

Beyond the rectory, over the stone bridge,
The band assembles, cardigans and gleaming brass,
Waits by the teashop and nursery gardens;
A trombone has gone to the gents in the coach park.
Under the church tower, among those gaily
Shirted, I take my place, a sight-seer.

From its due angle the afternoon sunlight
Glances on us, the children in white and green,
The boys with rushes and the girls garlanded,
And on the gravemounds lies, autumnal almost.
The parishioners, in Sunday best, are ready
To move in procession. The Rush-bearing at Grasmere

Begins to parade toward the Rothay Hotel
Slowly; band, vicar, sidesmen, and choir,
With hesitant banners, the living, and the new-born
In perambulators gaudy with flowers.
Out of sight now, turning the corner, they'll return
A moment later, as they did last year.

What hymn is the band playing? They reappear,
The local dwellers followed by children,
Here and now, past and to be contained together;
Like the plain water that stumbles below
The bridge I stand on, keeping the bed of the stream,
So altering that it seems never to alter.

Cockermouth

Past castle, brewery, over a sandstone bridge,
A Midland Bank, 'Fletcher's Fearless Clothing',
And huge effigy of an assassinated politician,
You come upon a Georgian grand frontage,

Still the town's 'big house', built for a Sheriff,
Not long ago ransomed from demolition
(The site an ideal one for the new bus-station)
And looked at, now, by a small bust of Wordsworth.

Turn down its by-lane leading to the river,
You'll see, fenced like a P.O.W. camp, reached by
An iron footbridge, the town's factory;
There ran a millrace, where was once a meadow,

And Derwent shuffles by it, over stones.
And if you look up the valley toward Isel
With Blindcrake to the north, cloudcatcher fells,
Whose waters track past here to Workington.

Eighteenth-century, like some town of Portugal;
Doorways faced with stone, proportionate windows,
And painted black and white, or gayer colours;
A scale perfectly kept, appropriately small.

Born here or hereabouts then: John Dalton,
Propounder of atomic theory; Fletcher
Christian; and, juxtaposing that Bounty mutineer,
Wordsworth the poet, of all unlikely men.

Tombs of shipmasters on the hill overlook
Town roofs, the valley where the river slips away
Toward the dead ports and the Irish sea,
Dowsed furnaces, closed mines of haematite

And coal, fortunes of Lowther and Curwen;
Slagheaps, the mansions of industrialists
Shuttered and rotting, burned or derelict,
Where a prosperity of impoverishment

Flourished, and now stands memorial
There, and in small classic façades of this town,
To the era designated Augustan;
Brown leaves about the baroque headstones fall.

On one side foundries; and the other way
Those frugal, delectable mountains
Where the smallholder yeoman, an anachronism,
Hung on into the nineteenth century.

So set, equidistant between past and future,
What more likely than, just here and then,
Should have been born that Janus-headed man,
A conservator and innovator

As the machine began to gather power,
Menacing nature to smile, because subdued?
The walled garden of his childhood
Stands as it was, pondering the river.

Five Songs

Stream

This young water
In my young day
Nosed like a hound
Through the meadow.

Changing, scarcely
Changed, it winds
Through Gloucestershire,
The Windrush stream.

Winds in a changeless
Image a
Recalling eye
Throws to the mind.

Mine is what's gone,
Not what's to come;
Then, I lived now,
Now, I live then.

Moon

O up there, zero
Shape illumining
These hills, and that lake –
Puller of water,

Puller of blood, blind
Eye not looking, but
There, opaque, a ball:
Have seen you over

A dead roofscape of
Human sleep; wondered
Why you beat so still.
Even the mobile

Windy surface of
Ocean seems, under
The quiet metal
Of that refracted

Lambency, gorgon
Struck.
      Now have seen how,
Soft as a fruit,

Our blueveined mother
The warm, appalling
Earth rises, vapoury,
Over your shoulder.

Valley

Valley of rock and snow,
The coarse grass burned yellow.

Hide, rib-cage, a hollow
Ram's horn. Here eagles flew.

The white ropes of water
Dangle from a black scar.

That road leads to the sea
Where ships in harbour lay.

The Roman tuba blew,
Glinted. An echo here.

River

A certain place
A stretch of time
Or water. Here
In summer I

Float on its arm.
Mountain, air, cloud!
A bowl of stone
And light! Like a

Fish this river
Slips from under
Me and these. The
Stone brow ever

There may follow,
Even the sky.
For, burly with
Rain, sinewy

And grainy streams,
The flood eludes
Old bounds, and hawks
At a tree-root.

Mountain

An outjutment
Where a slow bald
Swell of moorland
Declines. Old bone,

Old stone bone, wind
Beater still, still
There, in cloud or
Under snow, a

Waterbitten
Old mountain, stone
Obstruct. Cohere
Old rock, black slate!

Water can break
Granite: softest
Beat hardest, but
Not this mountain.

The mountain is
Rooted in bog, and
Glittering water.

Here below, bogrush,
Ragged robin, streams
Quick with fish. Heavy
Winged herons flap off

And a thumping hare
Tacks through white grass. What
Antithetical
Short stir, softness.

Cold now, cloudshrouded
Helmet of wind, a
Congealed mud, oldest
Rock, almost deaf as

Starlight. The light turf,
Scabbed lichen, cracked stone,
Holding a sky up.

Notes on a Visit
November 1976

Arrival

I landed at Jan Smuts at noon;
A cousin met, and drove me home;
The early summer smiled
Where I was born, and am exiled;
Green willows wept, jacarandas
Blew over windy verandas
While morning glory crept
Up pergola and parapet
Whose engardened villas slant
White roofs below Witwatersrand,
The suburbs of an earlier time,
Once gimcrack, now uncertain.
Uncertainty's what I read
Upon those tatty and beloved
Arcades of bottle stores and fruit
Merchants, pharmacists, estate
Agents, dog beauty parlours, and
Italian delicatessens,
The bioscope, half derelict,
And flyblown cafes that sell ostrich
Biltong as well as Coca Cola,
Pavements of dust and torn paper.
Yet I see no change in the day:
The black and gentle passers-by
As if they had no use for anger
Still greet with courtesy the stranger.
Only the human silhouette
Offered as a revolver target
In the sports-outfitter's window
Remembers June in Soweto.

Panorama

From the glassed fiftieth floor
Of the city's tallest tower
East, north, west, and south you see
Spread like a map, its history;
The koppies where white waters ran,
Railway and spoilheap, mine and dam;
The glittering highrisers, and
Almost below the horizon
A shadow city, the shadow
Of and over what we are;
The doll's-house roofs of Soweto,
A machine for not living in.

Nocturne

At midnight in the city, where
Nothing's left familiar
In any street except its name,
Kerk, Eloff, Loveday, Jeppe, Plein,
And, unreminded of a past,
Our century defines itself
In ferroconcrete, shining glass,
Dead edges that dehumanize,
Only the uncitizens
Are strollers-by on the pavements.
Those who need no pass, pass by
In shut vehicles, shut away
From their countrymen and city.
Patterned towers prick the night
With rigid flowerings of light
Frugal as Chinese painting; lit
Verticals loft cells of colour,
And headlights swarm like bees below.
Now the driver slows the car,
Points at a silent skyscraper,
Unlit windows hold it silent:

'That's where they keep prisoners
In solitary confinement.'
'Anyone there that you know?'
'There are kids there from Soweto.'
Electric as America,
The city sparkles like a sea;
The Hertzog Tower, slim and white
As a minaret, glints with light.

A look north

Twin highways to Pretoria
Dividing with their double scar
The highveld, point to the patria
Potestas ruling countrymen
Strangers, black and white and brown
Each in his own land a stranger.

Black poet

I met him in a room with more
Books in it than furniture.
What was it we had in common?
Each of us was Jo'burg born;
The same language that gave him
Words for verse had served my turn.
Humane, in himself consistent,
The eye and brow magnanimous,
His words quiet, few, and meant,
And his quality, gravitas;
Each of us the wrong colour,
He for now, I in future,
Each disabled by a skin.
Where I shall never be he's been,
His world is locked close to me
Although, as now, he enters mine;
Both natives of the one country,
I have been made, like him, alien.

Weather report

Thunder masses in the air
Northward, toward Pretoria;
The sun, about to disappear,
Sharp on the sun-coloured bricks
Of a long slab, the police barracks,
Throws a black shadow of some trees.
Oude Meester brandy in my glass,
I contemplate a summer
Storm assembling. Heavier
Cumuli range a fading sky.
The sun rolls under suddenly.
Has the night come, or the storm?
A flicker-crackle of lightning
Illumines a falling curtain,
Rain spilling on Magaliesberg
From the burst belly of a cloud.
'How fast the darkness falls,' we say.
'There's no twilight in Africa.'

Beeches

An old lady sits in a high veranda
That overlooks trees grown tall, sown in her time,
And thinks of trees a hemisphere away
Eighty years ago, when she was not sixteen.

'The men who came to shear my father's sheep
Would rest beneath two beeches when I brought
Their tea and scones beside the Annan water.
Beautiful trees. The man who owned the field,

Needing the money, had the beeches felled.
I never felt the same about the place.'
She looks toward Pretoria and the north
With fading eyes, recalling trivia,

While present shapes, tall eucalypti, yield
To an unfading and interior scene:
A river, with two beeches in a field,
Startles again, immortal to one mind.

Images for a Painter
i.m. Patrick Swift 1927-1983

I never imagined I
Should write your elegy.
I look out of the window
As you taught me to do.
All creation is grand.
Whatever is to hand
Deserves a line, praising
What is for being.

Thus at Westbourne Terrace
In long ago days
Brush in hand I'd see you
At your morning window
Transfer the thousand leaves
Of summer heavy trees
And delighting light
To another surface
Where they will not turn
With the turning season
But stay, and say
This is the mystery!
Or you would repeat
In pencil or in paint
The old stuffed pheasant too
That lived in your studio
Among the jars of turps
With a visiting ghost,
Charles Baudelaire's photo.
All the eye lights on
There for delighting.
Or put it this way,
A thing of beauty
Is joy perceived.
So you would give
Thanks for what is:
All art is praise.

Ah, those mornings
In many-hilled
Pombaline Lisbon!
The roads we travelled!
I do not mean
Only in Portugal –
Though now recalling
How, somewhere near
The river Guadiana
Going to Alcoutim,
We stopped the car
For, winding down
Round hills and bare,
Over no road came
The muleback riders
And blackshawled women
On foot, following
A coffin to nowhere:
Memento mori!

Or recollect
– Each one of us unique –
Your head suddenly
Thrown back, oblique
Eye over the laughter:
An aslant look
As if to say
Did the joke carry? The
Underlaid irony
Over the joke?

I see now
Out of my window
Mist rising from
A leaden Eden
Drifting slowly
Under trees barely
Leaved to the ford.
Gentle and aloud
The water breaks

As white as bread
Over the under road.
On the far bank
A field with trees
Each standing naked
On a fallen dress,
Brown and gold leaves.
I might relate
How swift my friend
Has gone, like these!
But I will not.
No cause for sadness,
You reader of Aquinas,
And clear Horace.
Whom the gods love, die
Young but not easily.

Prospects

I

Standing on Tara with Kavanagh
Wrapped in an old raincoat like
A scarecrow giant, and reminded
Of the other hill, Phaestos in Crete,
Of vastness and accurate light,
Though here the horizon is mist
And the wind is wet as Ireland;

It's somehow the same panorama,
Wide as the world is commonplace,
And ordinary as sacred;
The living, dead, romantic ghosts
Inhabiting the expressionless
Are genii loci here to lend a
Mirror to material nature.

I'd seen and thought the same upon
A high and Roman outpost set
Against the shoulder of Hardknott
Over the valley of the Esk,
With mountain following mountain
From wilderness to wilderness,
And tourist beercans in the grass.

Man is the measure, after all;
Distances are not curbed, but are
Fed and augmented by a wall,
Homestead or field; which remind us
The human being is central
To an indefinite universe
In which the earth is superstar.

It's twenty years or more since I
Stood on that royal windy hill;
Kavanagh cursing in the rain,
And not to be appeased until

We drove away in an old banger
In good time for the pub at Slane –
'No, it's your round,' – 'Black was the day

I met ye!' And the glasses fill.
Then back to Dublin and McDaid's,
A world that then seemed eternal,
But was ramshackle as our lives;
More fragile, even, as I find.
So many friends, so many graves.
I rake the ashes; last year's snows.

II

'Beth ware' – the doctor ends his tale –
'For no man woot whom God wol smyte.'
These were the very words I read
With no more thought than all was well;
Next day, three hundred miles away,
I stood by a hospital bed
In unbelief that he must die

His work half done: that Patrick Swift
With so much given, not yet old...
The spring was brilliant, not a cloud
In the March sky, and not a breath
Of wind disturbed the blue and gold
Day that lounged outside the glass
Pane where the world and living was.

Unlike and like as fingerprints
That never quite repeat a pattern,
We are, each one of us, in vision
And interpretation of what is,
Unique: a singular creation.
And yet with each a future dies
For more than for the dying one,

And even a past petrifies
When no new course or action can
Complete or modify what's been.
By that bed, in the banal sun,
There fell to me such thoughts as these.
In the renewal of the spring
I knew at heart no thing renews.

It took a year for him to die:
He had a year and more of grace,
Of sun and air; could even write
That all he looked upon was blessed;
And, looking at his canvases,
Convolute fig and almond groves
Set there by him, I know it was.

I said goodbye before he went.
That was the year when all was changed,
As changed as Algarve where he lived,
The once incommutable land
Bevilla'd, strung with golf courses,
With topless beaches, discothèques,
And fish and chips on every hand.

I'm in his tower studio
Where an Atlantic light comes in,
His easel set, dust gathering
Over the palette even now.
The figures of his forbears loom
From an unfinished landscape, half
Emergent, destined to remain

Shadows in a shadowy Wicklow:
The old ones, standing by their farm,
Must wait to be defined by him.
My friend, who cannot move his arm,
Or climb the tower stairs again,
Is breathing in a lower room,
And waiting for the light to go.

And as before, while the light fades,
We drink and speak; not as before:
For all we have to say is said,
Implicit in our being here.
And as we cannot look ahead,
Look back to find good fortune there:
The being that we both enjoyed

Which he can celebrate no more,
Or honour with reflecting hand.
Without his eyes I revisit
The cork oak forests of Monchique
That, stripped of bark above spring flowers,
Attend a far off Atlantic
Crawling to the Americas

Past the stone headland of Sagres.
Here is the café the forester
Sang like a lark in, while we ate
Partridges bedded in garlic
And drank Bemparece from Lagoa;
Here, Edwardian and embowered,
The gloomy purple-windowed spa

Dying in decorum and shade.
Or I look back at London years,
Talk of our scattered evenings –
MacDiarmid, Stevie, Kavanagh,
The Roberts, Barkers, and Behans,
Aleatory encounters
In Dean Street and in Fulham Road.

As for him, if he cannot speak,
As for me, if I cannot hear,
It's none the less a dialogue:
Between us the converse is clear.
For as his eye dulls or relumes
A legible response is there,
And I can read it at a glance.

III

Not two months later he was dead:
And swift as waves break on the shore
Was followed by another death,
My mother's, in her hundredth year.
Too long a life for me to mourn
A love too great, like a gold chain
Too rich, too heavy to be borne.

And all I feel is, I am free.
If only I were not her son
Her sacrifice – but then I am;
Inhibited from fathoming
What I well know she did for me.
I move to the familiar room
Lit by a wintry August sun

Where she no longer is, although
The Magaliesberg mountain line
Still defines, framed in her window,
A built-up highveld's horizon;
Her absent presence manifest
Among inanimate bric-à-brac,
Her furniture, my photograph

Which I, first thing I do, take down –
That small boy in a floppy hat
She loved, whom I abominate –
And feel, as if I'd switched it off,
The life extinguish in the room.
It's the first change. You can't change back.
I knew, that moment, she had gone.

And gone with her, what histories
Obliterate, and characters
Legible only to her long
Remembering, finally consign

To dark and nowhere with her mind?
Snuffed out, what ghosts are at an end,
Gone with their last rememberer?

I am to take the ashes home.
Where are they? In a suitcase there.
And she will lie by Annan water,
By an ornate Victorian tomb
Beside her father and her mother,
And neighbour to the rufous sandstone
Provincial burgh she grew up in

But eluded ever after.
I look at her photograph, taken
Perhaps a week before she died,
Dressed elegantly for a wedding,
And, leaning over her, the bride:
Life, to the last, was for enjoying.
'I feel I should apologize

Like Charles II,' so she wrote
To me, 'to take so long in dying.'
And then there is a shopping list
Made out on what was her last morning:
'Be sure you bring me, when you come,
The brandy and face-powder, Helen.'
And here's the bottle, which I open.

When Jocomina Tsukulu
Rang her: 'The Madam is departing
From this life,' Helen found her dead,
Her eyes closed by the African.
'I wouldn't have known what to do.
These Africans, of course they know
All about death,' as Helen said:

Thus the last service was performed
By the true unacknowledged friend
Part loved, part hated, part abused,
With whom she quarrelled to the end,

Without whom she could not have lived,
And by whom was understood,
But whom she did not understand.

Which goes for me, and all of us.
I'll not see Africa again
I think. So before going home
I take the highroad for a last
Look at the land where I was born:
And, driving north by Pilgrim's Rest
– A tin-walled gold prospector's town

Nudged in a kloof behind the Berg's
Blind granite stonecliffs from whose verge
You spy, two thousand feet below,
The lowveld endless as a sea
Stretch flatly till it meets the sky
Or the sky meets it – finally
I end up in the Game Reserve

Where beasts are cared for better than
My fellow-townsmen, whose bare plots
And mud shacks make a desert of
The nowhere they are banished in.
But I've been lucky with my skin;
Am able therefore to admire
The thousands of the impala,

Of zebra, sable, wildebeeste;
The ambling mastheads of giraffe,
And blunt, topheavy elephant
Browsing on treetops black with drought;
Or wingbeat of a hovering
Kingfisher with downbent beak
Intent above a shallow river.

Fenced in by homo sapiens,
The multiplicity of creation
Surviving in this museum Eden
And daily gaped at from machines,

Is counter to the actual
And outside world, the one we've made
A nightmare of, to service greed.

But should we blame intelligence?
We do not know what is to be
Any more than these innocent
And unpitying beasts of prey,
Or fleet birds and horned ruminants
That live for the indifferent day
And neither fear nor hope tomorrow's.

IV

Here is as far as I shall go –
A bluff above Olifants River
Looking toward the Lebombo
Mountains where the sun rises over
Bushveld as level as a table,
As vatic a panorama
As Phaestos or the hill of Tara:

Thus I am back where I began.
Perched on a cliff, the rondavel
I sleep in overlooks the sand
Bed of the Olifants below
That nourishes a foliage
Which is the brown land's only green,
And brings the kudu here to graze.

An historyless primeval
Wilderness with no memories,
With not a myth or ghost or fable,
Whose retrospects are yet to come.
I watch the sun, a bloody eyeball,
Climb up and clear the mists of morning
That blear a prospect of nothing,

Africa, tabula rasa!
Resolved upon no resolution
I pack my bag, and throw away
Souvenirs of too short a stay –
Let them take the next comer in!
And turn to trace the road I came
From illusion to illusion.

> *Patrick Kavanagh, 1909-1967*
> *Patrick Swift, 1927-1983*
> *Jean Murray Wright, 1881-1983*

An Elegy
Phillipa Reid 1927-1985

These verses you will never read,
For you, beloved friend, are dead.
Under a mountain, by a lake,
Your ashes for my ashes wait.
I have been silent for too long,
Dumbstruck by that oblivion
I am to share and never know.
Beloved, it is high summer now,
Your roses blowing, each petal
Consummate and ephemeral,
Emblems of joy you and I,
Two persons in the one body,
So often granted to each other.

But I look back to that October
And ordinary autumn morning,
The air and banal sunlight glowing;
You sit upon a kitchen chair
Abstracted. Then you are not there.
An absence slowly apparent:
The body moves, and you aren't in it.

★

As ephemeral as a rose
The art, the vocation that chose
Her from the ruck, to illumine
What we are, can be, or have been:
A voice, a body on a stage
To define, interpret, appraise
With passion correlative
To the perception of what is;
Art living in a living now
With nothing but recall to show
At curtain call, performance over,
The solidity of a sculpture
For ever valid, even though

Made for the moment, made for now,
Conterminous as that rose,
And fading as a moment fades.

A last chat in the hospital,
A brave face and frightened eye:
It breaks my spirit to recall
That goodbye, casual and final.
Then nine days' coma, to awake
Unable to so much as speak,
But hearing, understanding all.
The long blind corridors I trod,
And ghastly pavements glinting rain,
That fardel of a hopeless hope –
'Technically successful, the op.,
But –.' Never to come back again.

'Love at first sight' – no, never that;
But for me, when our glances met
That Sunday in Lamb's Conduit Street,
Half-guessing at what lay ahead,
I recognized the other half
Of what I'd be, not what I was,
Brought by a destiny or good luck.

Today, the 24 July,
Her birthday. I recall the first
We shared – it was her twenty-fourth –
The packet, Dieppe-Newhaven,
Butting across a windy Manche
With us on board her, en retour
From castle-building days in Spain
Where she had given her promise
To waste it for the sake of mine:
Unselfseeking, too generous
To win that token, token fame.
All I could give was happiness,
A happiness she did not want,
Preferring the acknowledgement
Of anon, an audience.

What she gave me was all she had,
Was it then nothing, that I gave?
You get no answer from the dead,
You cannot parley with a grave.

And all that's left is memory.
I cannot visualize her face.
Here is her image on a leaf
Of paper, freeze-dried from the life,
A shadow; and she is a shade.

And there are letters; shadows too
Of an accord. Two minds, but one
Enjoyment of reality:
A making light of common day,
Oblique, ironic perception
Of aboriginal comedy.

So many gifts, except for one
Which in the end annulled them all:
Virtuosity; natural skill;
A naked body's perfection;
Intelligence, that illumines
And illustrates the beautiful;
Courtesy, courage, compassion,
All these, bar the one gift not given,
Ever unlucky, of good fortune.

Half of me, as I know, is gone,
And more than half; see what a swathe
The winter cut! So few are left
Of those who made me what I am.
It is another ambience
I now live in, although the same
River my window under dawdles,
The same thrush props about the lawn
Marauding; the same chaffinch startles.
I know it is not her I mourn,
It is myself, a lost I am.